EUROPA ✦ MILITAI
SPECIAL N°11

NAPOLEON'S LINE INFANTRY and ARTILLERY

RECREATED IN

COLOUR PHOTOGRAPHS

STEPHEN E. MAUGHAN

Windrow & Greene

Dedication:
For my parents, Edward and Elizabeth.

This edition published
in Great Britain 1997 by
Windrow & Greene Ltd
5 Gerrard Street
London W1V 7LJ

Designed by John Anastasio/Creative Line
Printed in Great Britain by
Amadeus Press Ltd, Huddersfield

A CIP catalogue record for this book is
available from the British Library

ISBN 1 85915 053 5

Acknowledgements:
I would like to thank the many re-enactors who gave
generously of their time to enable the photographs in
this book to be taken. In my previous book in this
series, "Napoleon's Line Cavalry", I mentioned that we
had driven almost 10,000 miles and taken nearly 3,000
photographs. Having covered several more events the
total is now over 13,000 miles and around 5,000
photographs - a single trip to Jena represented 2,000
miles - and the saga continues. . . I would also like to
thank the staff of Colorworld Ltd, North Shields, for
their help and speed in processing the material
included in this book; and Colin Worley of Worley
Publications & Booksellers, who searched diligently,
and usually successfully, for several obscure books. As
in almost any book on the uniforms of this period,
author and editor wish to record their great debt to the
published researches of Philip Haythornthwaite.

   A limited edition print run (10ins x 8ins) of each of the
photographs in this book is available from: Five Star
Photography, 34 North Lodge Terrace, Darlington,
Co.Durham DL3 6LY, England - prices on application.

Contact addresses:

British Napoleonic Association
Michael Freeman
5 Thingwall Drive
Irby, Wirral
Merseyside L61 3XN
England

9eme Léger
Martin Lancaster
11 Loring Place
Whetstone
London N20 0UJ
England

21eme de Ligne
Chris Durkin
22 Swallow Street
Oldham
Lancashire OL8 4LD
England
(Also contact for
information exchange
service.)

La Garde Impériale
George Lubonski
10 Skipton Road
Silsden BD20 9JZ
England

127eme de Ligne
Gunter Franke
Lütjen Marschweg 33a
25704 Meldorf
Germany

Feldregiment Bevilaqua
Tobias Reh
Uranusstr. 28
04205 Leipzig
Germany

18eme de Ligne
Jörg Nogohsek
Utenbacherstr. 34
99510 Apolda
Germany

La Grande Armée
Regis Surmont
2 rue de Mai
1945 59215 Abscon
France

Napoleon's Infantry

Following the Revolution the French infantry of the *ancien régime* were transformed. The rigidly disciplined regiments of long-service professionals, drilled to perform complex Frederickian manoeuvres, were replaced after 1791 by a more flexible force capable of assimilating a mass of rapidly enlisted and virtually untrained civilian volunteers and conscripts. The old powers of Europe were determined to strangle the Revolution before its infection spread; and in this crisis France needed willing cannon-fodder more urgently than military sophistication.

The brilliant Lazare Carnot - "the organiser of victory" - was elected to the Committee of Public Safety with responsibility for military affairs in August 1793, when invasion and revolt threatened on all sides. A week later universal conscription was introduced - the *levée en masse* - which made every able-bodied man in France potentially liable for military service. (Its introduction at this time of revolutionary and patriotic fervour lent the system an aura of legitimacy, from which Napoleon would later profit when building armies for his wars of conquest.) Untrained conscripts bolstered Gen. Houchard's army to 42,000 men and enabled him to repulse the Duke of York's 13,000 troops at Hondschoote that September, and then the Prince of Orange's forces at Menin.

Despite his victories a later failure would send Houchard to the guillotine, where Gen.Custine had already suffered a Revolutionary close shave after his failure at Valenciennes in May 1793. Among an aristocratic officer class already traumatised by the Reign of Terror the pernicious practice of executing unsuccessful commanders did nothing for initiative or loyalty; when Gen.Dumouriez had felt the shadow of the guillotine fall across him after a defeat in January he had fled to the Allies, calling the incumbent French government a collection of "three hundred scoundrels and four hundred imbeciles". Carnot was influential in protecting professional officers from revolutionary savagery, and in promoting the competent among them who were willing to continue to serve their country under the democratic title of "citizen". (The future Marshals Davout and Grouchy were among those who did, to Napoleon's later benefit.)

In 1793-94 an offical programme of "amalgamation" was instituted by Carnot. The old regiments were replaced by numbered *Demi-Brigades* each of three battalions; the 2nd, which formed a central base of fire and manoeuvre, was a trained regular unit, with newly raised 1st and 3rd battalions of conscripts or volunteers forming attack columns on its flanks, where sheer mass and impetus might succeed in the absence of discipline or skill at arms. This *ordre mixte,* alternating covering fire with aggressive assault, would be essentially unchanged throughout the Napoleonic Wars and at every level from battalion to division.

When the frontiers of France were secure the Convention now directing the fortunes of the Revolution went onto the offensive, and from May 1794 the new armies won a string of victories in the Low Countries, on the Rhine, in the Alps and on the Mediterranean coast. In March 1796 the 26-year-old Gen.Napoleon Bonaparte, a former artillery officer who had distinguished himself against a British and Royalist force at Toulon in 1793, took up command of the scattered, hungry, ill-equipped and hangdog Army of Italy. First he fed them; then he led them to repeated victories over the Austrians in a lightning campaign which established him as France's leading general, and as a charismatic leader of men.

In 1798 the Directory (as the government was by now renamed) was not sorry to agree to his plan to sail away to occupy Egypt as a bastion against Britain's global strategy. Despite Bonaparte's victories over the Mamelukes and Turks, Admiral Nelson's destruction of the French fleet left the Army of the Orient stranded and essentially irrelevant. Developments in Europe became more urgent; and in autumn 1799 he abandoned his army to its fate, slipping back to Paris. This would be the first of several demonstrations of the cold ruthlessness behind his rhetorical style of leadership; yet although some attacked him as a deserter, his public popularity survived.

Gen.Bonaparte became First Consul of France after usurping power in a coup on 18 *Brumaire* (9 November)

1799; just 30 years old, he was the victor of more than a dozen battles in less than four years. After further triumphs over Austrian armies in Italy he crowned himself as Napoleon I, Emperor of the French, in 1803. For more than a decade he would rule as a military dictator, astonishing the world with his conquests and redrawing the map of Europe.

His instrument would be one of history's most formidable hosts - the *Grande Armée*. At the head of this army he crushed the Austrians and Russians in the brilliant Austerlitz campaign of 1805, and the vaunted Prussians at Jena and Auerstädt in 1806. Checked by the Russians at Eylau in February 1807, he smashed them at Friedland in June, forcing both Russia and Prussia to accept terms which left him the master of most of Continental Europe. By sea Britain was invulnerable; she continued to bankroll Continental alliances against Napoleon, but was unable to intervene by land in any strength.

In 1809 the Austrians rose against France again, and inflicted his first major defeat on Bonaparte at Aspern-Essling that May. He had his revenge at Wagram in July, forcing Austria to submit once again. In 1810 Napoleon and his armies stood at the pinnacle of their reputation.

Their tactics, even their uniforms were copied by many of their one-time adversaries, now satellites or enforced allies. Only Britain - still fighting on patiently, sustaining Wellington's small (and to Napoleon's marshals, irritatingly indestructible) army in Spain and Portugal - championed a different tactical doctrine, which was to prove admirably effective against the French system.

One central pillar of Napoleon's system of command, and probably the only true survival of the Revolutionary spirit during his regime, was his willingness to promote for proven merit at all levels. Another was his encouragement of every branch of the service to think of itself as something special, distinguished by gorgeous uniforms and particular emblems. Though deeply cynical about "spending" his conscripts' lives in pursuit of his dreams, he was a superbly compelling motivator of soldiers *en masse,* and mesmerising face to face. Under the old Royalist regime the highest a common soldier could rise in the ranks was sergeant. Under the Empire, at least in theory, anyone could be promoted as high as their talent or merit would take them.

In the Bourbon army it had taken Michel Ney, the son of a barrel-cooper from the Moselle, four years to rise to the rank of corporal-quartermaster; in the four years between 1792 and 1796 he rose from second lieutenant to general; by 1804 he was a marshal, soon to be a duke, and would die a prince. Napoleon harnessed the spirit of meritocracy which had first flourished under the Revolution and incorporated it into his new Legion of Honour; he advanced the successful, showering them with titles and riches, for as he said, "It is by baubles and titles that men are led". He exerted the same spell over the soldiers *en masse,* presenting them with dramatic standards and picking out individuals for reward; they repaid him by surging forward over a score of bloody fields with cries of *"Vive l'Empereur!"*

It was often said that Napoleon owed everything to his Line troops, yet gave all the praise and glory to his Imperial Guard. The only consolation that Line soldiers could take from this was the knowledge that if they lived long enough and performed their duties well, they too might aspire to the pay and privileges of Guard status; the Guard were selected from among Line troops of proven courage and discipline. This was probably little comfort to many a young conscript who had been drawn into the Napoleonic adventure by no more than an inability to afford the purchase of a replacement to stand in for him.

The uniforms which these unfortunate youths received were less than glamorous as first issued. The diarist Captain Elézar Blaze asked "If a person wished to devise a more inconvenient method of clothing the soldier, could he have hit upon one more to the purpose?" He describes the grotesque figure that a young conscript could cut in ill-fitting breeches and gaiters which fell down about his heels. "For this dress a man should be well built, well made; he ought to have legs furnished with fair protuberances. A man of twenty is not yet formed - nay, we were joined by conscripts who were under nineteen. This accoutrement gave them an absolutely silly look; by contrast, it sat extremely well on the Imperial Guard, which never fought unless in full dress, but which fought very rarely." Blaze was right about the gaiters, even to the point of stating that the long campaign trousers were far superior to them (just ask any French Infantry re-enactor. . .)

In 1803 the old title *Régiment* once more replaced *Demi-Brigade*. By 1807 there were 31 Light Infantry regiments, and 89 Line Infantry regiments numbered between 1 and 112, with 23 regimental numbers vacant. (This may have been a deliberate attempt to give the impression that the French Army was larger than it was; in the battles of 1805 and 1806 France's enemies consistently overestimated her numerical strength.) Each regiment comprised between two and four battalions; and a battalion's theoretical strength was 1,042 officers and men, although a *chef de bataillon* considered himself lucky to have half these numbers actually present when on campaign.

LIGHT INFANTRY, c.1795

The old Royalist army had 12 battalions of Chasseurs to act as skirmishers ahead and on the flanks of the battle line. In 1793 the regular battalions were amalgamated with volunteers and conscripts (as with the Line units) into 22 new three-battalion *Demi-Brigades Légères.* By 1800 there were 30 Demi-Brigades, most of four battalions but some of two. Each battalion had eight companies of *chasseurs,* and one élite company of *carabiniers* - supposedly the picked men, equivalent to the *grenadier* company in Line units. Each company was supposed to have three officers, 12 NCOs and about 120 men; but during the Revolutionary Wars numbers varied hugely.

The recreated *9e Léger* follow the events of 200 years ago with dress appropriate to the year; e.g., for re-enactment events in 1997 they wear the uniforms of 1797. They made an exception for the 1995 Waterloo event, wearing shakos instead of helmets and bicorns.

(Above right) A corporal of the recreated *9e Demi-Brigade Légère* fires his musket while skirmishing.

(Right) In a bivouac outside the walls of Le Quesnoy, a northern French fortress restyled by Louis XIV's great engineer Vauban, a company marker flag - *fanion* - displays Republican and Light Infantry emblems.

A three-deep line of the 9th Light prepare to receive the enemy with their backs to the walls of Le Quesnoy. As Light Infantry regiments acquired élite status they were used more often in a close order role; in the campaigns of the Empire the tactical difference between Light and Line units almost disappeared.

The motley uniforms and variety of striped trousers made up from ticking material are taken from contemporary sources. In fact these soldiers are probably unusually smart; not for nothing were the ragged masses of Revolutionary soldiery called "sans-culottes" - "men without breeches".

(Above & left) This corporal of the 9e Demi-Brigade Légère has a rather superior example of the "Tarleton"-style leather helmet issued to the Light Infantry in 1791; his at least has a fur roach - many only had a stuffed cloth tube. It was not universal issue, some units retaining the old bicorn hat; nor was it much liked by many of those who did receive it, although the 9th kept theirs until at least 1798. Note the rudimentary "epaulette" of 18th century style - really just a fringed shoulder strap - in the green traditionally associated with light troops (the original Chasseur battalions had worn all-green uniforms), with a red "crescent" - a common variation among Light troops, hinting at élite status.

The armies of the 1790s had very makeshift logistics, and regulation 1793 uniform was often replaced by whatever came to hand. Although the corporal's clothing is entirely civilian apart from the helmet and uniform coatee, the latter conforms to the regulations: all dark blue except for red collar and cuff-flaps, with white metal buttons, white piping, lapels cut to a point at the bottom, the tail turn-backs decorated with the buglehorn emblem of the branch. His rank is identified by two diagonal stripes of white worsted braid on the forearms.

His field equipment is also complete - a black leather cartridge box and a combined frog for a bayonet and short sabre suspended by whitened leather crossbelts, and a cowhide knapsack.

The fanion is carried with its staff thrust down the barrel of his Charleville musket; it bears on this side the unit title and buglehorn corner badges.

(Left & below) The close-fitting 1791 Tarleton style helmet - which was also issued to Line units - was thought uncomfortable, and became sweaty and smelly in use. In one well-known episode the 46th Line gathered together and with due ceremony threw their helmets into a river, replacing them with felt bicorn hats privately purchased at 5 francs apiece. The soldier at left wears a privately acquired greatcoat. These were not an issue item before the end of 1805, and even then "cloth greatcoats were distributed to the army after Austerlitz, but since most of the cloth was obtained through requisitions made from the conquered territories one could see coats of all colours in the same unit, which made for a shockingly motley effect".

The early cowhide knapsack did not have leather retaining straps for a coat or blanket roll, so greatcoats had to be tied in place with string when not in use. At this date all ranks of Light units were officially to carry brass-hilted sabres (although they were not often available in sufficient numbers). The sabre had little practical value as a weapon, and apart from being a mark of status it was more useful for chopping firewood and other camp chores.

(Right) In a three-rank battle line like this, firing by files required the third rank to hold their fire and load, then pass muskets to the second rank. In practice, the third rank would become excited once battle commenced and would blaze away, often injuring their comrades in the middle and front ranks. Marshal St Cyr believed that 25% of all French battle casualties were inflicted in this way, especially as more and more raw conscripts filled the ranks thinned by costly campaigns. (Indeed, after the battles of Bautzen and Lützen in 1813 Napoleon believed that many conscripts' wounds were deliberately self-inflicted, and ordered draconian punishment for all showing certain sorts of wounds until persuaded, with some difficulty, that they could be innocently suffered.) Needless to say, the "leopardskin" turbans of the helmets had never been nearer to a leopard than a French abbattoir

(Above & above right) Revolutionary Wars Line and Light infantrymen at their ease, wearing the undress cap - *bonnet de police*. The former sports Republican emblems and slogans; and note the white coat lapels and waistcoat of the Line. The latter displays the white wool buglehorn of the Light troops, and wears the blue sleeveless waistcoat of that branch.

(Right & opposite) Light Infantry conscripts are drilled by a sergeant wearing white summer trousers and gaiters; the regulation legwear for the branch was dark blue breeches and short black gaiters cut and piped to resemble the shape of Hessian boots - note among the recruits both green and red gaiter piping, for chasseurs and carabiniers respectively. The sergeant (right, foreground) is distinguished by a silver sleeve stripe on red backing and epaulettes of mixed green and silver lace. Note the metal buglehorn emblem on his cartridge box lid.

Light Infantry training was supposed to be more thorough than that of the Line, since they had to perform more demanding tasks such as skirmishing in open order, dispersing to defend built-up areas, and acting as scouts.

Under the Consulate some 50,000 men per annum passed through the drill instructors' hands; by 1812 this had risen to about 280,000. In the early days subsitutes might be bought - men who would take the place of a called-up conscript - for between 2,000 and 4,000 francs; by 1813, after the disappearance of hundreds of thousands of men into the vast silence of Russia, the going rate was 12,000 francs, if the unhappy "Marie-Louise" could find anyone to take it. (For comparison, a pair of shoes was valued at 6 francs, a shirt at 4 francs.)

LIGHT INFANTRY, c.1805

(Left) The regulation pace was 76 steps per minute, but when marching at ease across country the soldiers would obviously set their own pace. The shako introduced in 1801 bore a buglehorn badge on the front, a plume or pompon and a cockade on one or either side, and green plaited cords with hanging tassels and *racquettes*. The chasseur companies officially wore blue shoulder straps piped white, but often sported fringed green epaulettes, sometimes with red or yellow "crescents"; cuff shapes also varied between regiments.

(Above right) A drummer, distinguished by white-edged red lapels and shoulder "wings", and red waistcoat. He wears the diamond-shaped 1806 shako plate, with the cockade and pompon now moved to the front.

(Above & right) A chasseur (left), his cockade fastened to the left side of the shako by a loop of yellow braid. The red sleeve chevrons are long service stripes. His veteran comrade is a pioneer - *sapeur;* each battalion had four serving with the carabiniers. This explains his red epaulettes; red lapels are a non-regulation touch typical of members of the battalion's *tête de colonne*. Traditionally bearded, he has a fur cap like the carabinier's dress headgear; note pioneer's crossed axe sleeve badges, and appied metal emblems backed with red on his crossbelts.

13

(Left, above left & above)
A field officer, his two fringed silver epaulettes marking a major or above, and his bi-metal gorget the fact that he is on duty. Other distinctions of officer status are the fancy silver lace top band of his shako, the long-tailed *habit* in place of the men's shorter-tailed coatee, silver-embroidered turn-back emblems, embroidered thigh knots on his tight breeches, and his sword. The Light Infantry regarded themselves as superior to the Line, and this élan was reflected in such light cavalry touches as the hussar-style boots.

(Left) Rear detail of coatee turn-backs, cartridge boxes and gaiters.

(Below) A sergeant wearing the universal type of infantry shako issued from 1806, with leather reinforcement chevrons on the sides, and on the front a pompon and a leather tricolour cockade above a diamond-shaped plate. Officially this bore a crowned eagle and buglehorn badge, but many variations are recorded. Protective metal scales on the chinstrap were not yet official issue, but individuals are known to have added them. Note again the silver sleeve stripe and mixed green and silver epaulettes of this rank. Note also the white stitching on the collar; matching coloured thread was not yet used.

LINE INFANTRY, c.1805

The dark blue habit had red-piped white lapels cut square at the bottom; white-piped red collar and cuffs - the latter showing many unit variations; and blue shoulder straps piped red. Buttons were of yellow metal. The cutaway coat was worn over a white long-sleeved waistcoat which doubled as a drill or fatigue jacket, white breeches, and black gaiters. The *fusiliers* had a single crossbelt supporting both cartridge box and frogged bayonet scabbard.

The felt bicorn - light and comfortable - bore a national cockade at left front. Pompons were starting to be worn in colour sequences identifying battalion or company, but these were not rigidly regulated.

Often the hair was still worn long, with queue and *cadenettes* (sidelocks), but styles might vary according to a commander's whim. The trend towards a shorter, hygienic cut - emphatically favoured by Napoleon - had already begun.

(Below, left to right:)
(1) Caporal, his rank marked by two sleeve stripes in *aurore* - peach/orange. Note waterproof campaign cover on the cartridge box flap, with painted regimental number.
(2) Fusilier from rear. The tail turnbacks are plain here; embroidered or appliqué emblems such as hearts, diamonds, stars or unit numbers were common, and after 1804 the Imperial eagle.
(3) Sergent, identified by a single gold sleeve stripe. Like the corporal he has a *sabre-briquet* on a second crossbelt to which his bayonet is also frogged, but with a mixed red/gold fist strap.
(4) Fusilier - note lapel shape. Individual choice of waistcoat colours is the sort of variation characteristic of the period.

The uniform worn pre-1806 evolved gradually from that of the 1793 regulations; its origins lay in that of the National Guard of the Revolutionary period.

Line regiments at this date had either three or four battalions. Each battalion comprised (from the official introduction of *voltigeurs* in September 1804) four companies of *fusiliers;* one of *grenadiers* - supposedly a shock force of the strongest men; and one of *voltigeurs* -a light company, supposedly made up of the most agile, intelligent marksmen for skirmishing duties. Each company was supposed to have three officers, a sergeant-major, four sergeants, a corporal-quartermaster, eight corporals, two drummers and 121 privates.

These recreated soldiers of the 18e de Ligne are smartly uniformed; despite many historical references to the unkempt appearance of the French Army on campaign, they were as capable as any

other contemporary army of a smart paradeground turn-out when in permanent quarters, such as the vast encampment at Boulogne where the Grande Armée prepared for an invasion of England in 1803-05. Nevertheless, in pre-industrial armies true uniformity in a modern sense was unknown, given dispersed manufacture, random shortages, and the still strong 18th century tradition of freedom in small regimental details.

(**Below & right**) Rear view details of equipment. The fusiliers' shoulder straps were cut in a three-pointed "duck's-foot" shape at the outer end and buttoned at the neck end; they secured the crossbelts to the shoulder. The knapsack now had provision for kit stowage straps - note the greatcoat folded in regulation style with the ends tucked in.

(Left) Two attractive angles on the pre-1806 uniform and field equipment. Note the red-tasselled forage caps rolled and strapped beneath the cartridge boxes.

(Opposite) When the size of a battalion dwindled below a certain point the three-rank firing line was replaced by two ranks in order to maintain the length of the battalion frontage. Writing during his final exile on St.Helena, Napoleon noted the weakness of the three-rank system: "The fire of the third rank is recognized as very imperfect, and dangerous to...the first two. One prescribed the first rank to place its knee on the ground in fire by battalion, and in voluntary fire the third rank loaded the muskets of the second... The infantry must be ranged in two ranks only, because the musket only permits this order."

(Inset) Cuff, buttons and sergeant's rank stripe.

(Left) Wooden clogs, stuffed with straw for insulation, were commonly worn in camp in order to save wear on the leather shoes, whose replacement was unpredictable; they are surprisingly comfortable.

(Above) Men of a grenadier company, distinguished by fringed red epaulettes, forming up; note at right centre a single voltigeur, with yellow epaulettes, cap braid and buglehorn badge. Their turn-out is fairly motley and their appearance relaxed; an easy familiarity often existed between soldiers and their NCOs, who shared the same backgrounds.

This re-enactment camp has neatly aligned streets of tents.

These were not general issue, and soldiers who wanted to sleep dry had to devise their own bivouacs. In the great military township outside Boulogne they excavated dug-outs in the chalky soil, roofed with timber and thatch (adequate in summer, but liable to flood in winter). The daily ration issue was limited to thin soup, a little meat and .75kg (1.5lbs) of bread; soldiers fished and gathered shellfish from the nearby Channel beaches, and created vegetable gardens in the camps (in some cases, complete with lawns!)

(Right) An order of February 1806 introduced shakos for the Line; they were already in use by Light Infantry. The

sheer scale of the necessary issue delayed their receipt by many units until 1807, and the great victories of 1806 were won by men still wearing the bicorn. The 1806 shako had a felt or covered cardboard body, waterproof leather top, leather headband and V-shaped side reinforcements and a leather peak. The diamond-shaped brass plate bore the Imperial eagle and the regimental number, and was surmounted a tricolour cockade and a woo pompon in company colours. Brass chinscales, attached by boss decorated with a star, we not yet official issue but were commonly fitted. The leather reinforcements and chinscales gave some protection against cuts and blows.

23

(**Left & above**) A decree of April 1806 ordered a reversion to white - the old Bourbon colour - for French Army uniforms. This was probably an economic decision, as the cost of the indigo dye used to create "French blue" had rocketed due to the effect of the British blockade on French ports. The Line regiments were divided into blocks of eight each issued with the same facing colour; the 17e to 24e wore scarlet. This sergeant of the 21e wears white summer campaign trousers over his white breeches and black gaiters; and his shako is protected by an oilcloth cover with a painted number.

In practice only a minority of regiments received white coats before the order was countermanded in May 1807. It was smart for parades, but in bivouac and on campaign it became filthy: "All the conscripts coming from France were clothed in the white uniform, which made a really unsightly mixture when they were put in units still wearing blue. It was a really odd idea to give white uniforms to troops destined to pass their time in bivouac; you should have seen how dirty those young recruits got!" In action, "The appearance of blood on the white coats made even the most trifling wound look serious." In November 1809 Suchet noted: "The medley is over - there are no more hats [bicorns], no more white coats."

(**Above & above right**)
The 1806 shako worn by
fusiliers of the recreated 45e
de Ligne, complete with the
white cords, tassels and
racquettes ("flounders") added
for parades.

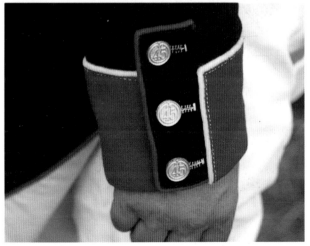

(**Right**) Detail of 45e
de Ligne cuff and buttons.

LINE INFANTRY, 1812

(Below, right & opposite) In January 1812 the so-called "Bardin" regulations introduced this new short-tailed *habit-veste,* with lapels cut square to the waist; and shortened black gaiters. For the fusiliers the colours of coatee details were unchanged, but the turn-back emblem was standardised as a blue crowned N.

The simplified 1810 pattern shako plate is worn by this sergeant of the 127e de Ligne, a German regiment raised in March 1811 during an expansion which brought several foreign units into the Line. The 127th was raised partly from men of the Hamburg and Lübeck Civil Guards and the Hanoverian Legion, partly from new conscripts and volunteers, with a mix of German and (mainly) French officers and NCOs. This sergeant wears the second crossbelt to support the sabre which was now a mark of NCO or grenadier company status only.

(Below right) The rear view of a corporal, on the march to the 127th's first duty as coastal garrison troops at Stade in October 1811, shows the rolled greatcoat bulked out by his having stowed personal effects or items of plunder inside it. Clogs and a small candle lantern have been strapped to his pack.

(OVERLEAF) The sergeant and a *caporal-fourrier* of the 127th. Note the crowned N turn-back emblem; and the company quartermaster-corporal's ranking: corporal's forearm stripes, plus a single gold stripe on the left upper sleeve only.

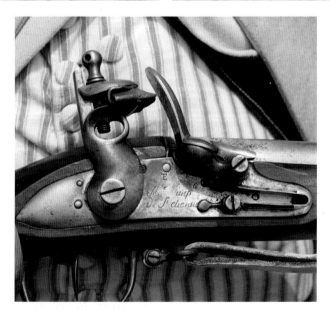

(Right) Lock of the 1777/1802 pattern Charleville flintlock musket. The weapon was 112.6cm (44.7in) long, with a bore of 17.5mm (.69in) - slightly longer and smaller respectively than the British Short Land pattern ("Brown Bess"). The lighter French ball had slightly less "windage" - the gap between the ball and the inside of the smoothbore barrel - and was propelled by a roughly equal powder charge; but there was no significant difference in accuracy - at 150 yards roughly half the balls fired might hit a formed-up regiment of enemy troops, but performance dropped off dramatically above that range.

Above left & above) The loading sequence; the drill manual actually distinguished 12 movements. First a paper cartridge holding powder and ball is taken from the box (which held about 50 rounds). The end is bitten off; a little powder is poured into the priming pan, which is then closed by the spring-loaded frizzen. The musket butt is grounded, and the rest of the powder poured down the barrel followed by the ball; the cartridge paper acts as a wad. The ramrod is taken from its "pipes" beneath the barrel, and used to tamp down the charge; it is then returned to its housing.

(Right) The musket is loaded, and the fusilier awaits the order to present. For safety this man still has the cock, holding the wedge of flint which will ignite the charge when it falls to strike the frizzen, pulled only half way back - thus the phrase "half-cock". When firing repeated volleys in battle two to three rounds a minute was considered a fair rate of fire.

(Above left) The fusilier presents his musket; he will now thumb back the cock, and pull the trigger.

(Above) A voltigeur fires. The flint knocks the frizzen up, exposing the priming pan and dropping sparks into it. The priming flares, making him flinch.

(Left) Sparks from the priming pass through the touchhole to ignite the main charge, enveloping him in thick white smoke.

At point blank range it was easy to fire high,

32

specially during *feu de*
pillebaude - the confused
period of "firing at will" which
followed the breakdown of
volley discipline in battle. Gen.
Brack recommended that at
close range a man should aim
at the belly; at 100 paces, the
chest; at 130, the shoulders; at
170, the head; and at 195, the
hat plume.

(Right) If all else failed, the
Napoleonic soldier had his
bayonet. The French pattern
was 45.6cm (18in) long, with
a tapering triangular section
blade. The socket fitted over
the muzzle and fixed with a
locking ring, but veterans also
used to tie it on with string for
extra security. French *élan*
with the bayonet was
legendary; but in fact, the
success or failure of most
assaults at bayonet point were
decided before contact was
made, when the nerve of one
side or the other broke.

(Below right) To keep the
flintlock musket in action
required frequent attention.
Every soldier carried - handy
on a chain or lace from a
buttonhole - an *épinglette* or
pricker. Burnt black powder
quickly built up in the barrel
and around the priming pan,
and after a few shots the
encrusted fouling could block
the touchhole if it was not
pricked clean. (We also read of
men urinating down the barrel
in order to scour out the burnt
powder.) The flint itelf -
wrapped here in a piece of
leather to prevent it from
shattering under the pressure of
the cock's screw jaws - needed
frequent replacement. It could
wear unevenly, chipping its
edge or even breaking up from
repeated impact on the steel
frizzen. Every soldier had to
carry spare flints in his pouch.

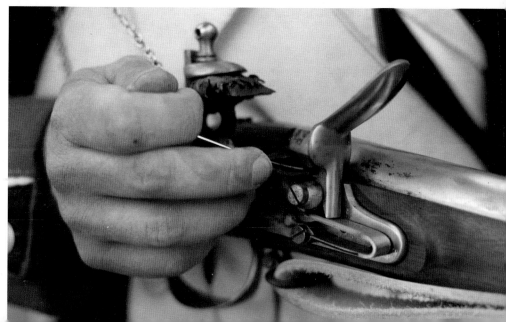

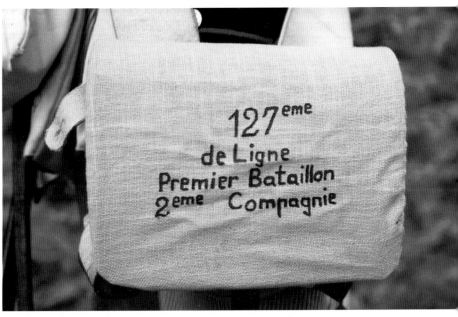

(Above & above right)
The 127th on campaign, wearing loose trousers. The regiment used shako covers made of hessian, stamped with the number; cheap and easy to make, they protected the more expensive shako, its plate and other furniture from the elements, and had a let-down rain flap.

The three battalions of Col. Backar's 127th had a total strength of 46 officers and 1,366 men when, in June 1812, they reached the Niemen during the advance into Russia. By the time they reached Moscow the figure was 28 officers and 465 men. Just 16 officers and 67 men returned from Russia, still carrying their Eagle.

127eme de Ligne Premier Bataillon 2eme Compagnie

(Below) Reconstruction of the straight-lasted shoes of the Napoleonic infantryman - i.e. they are identical, not made specifically for left or right feet. When worn they soon take on the contours of the foot, so to prevent uneven wear men were supposed to change feet regularly. In fact, what they needed on the march was comfort, and once a shoe was "bedded in" it was often worn on one foot only.

For an infantry army a supply of good shoes was vital; the memoirs are full of instances of men hobbling along with their bloody feet wrapped in rags. Each man was supposed to have two spare pairs, but in fact this was a very rare luxury. When Gen. Duhesme needed shoes for his troops detachments were sent with a corporal's guard to requisition them from the civil population, calling at every house "without respect of class or business" until they had assembled 10,000 pairs.

(Above) Detail showing how the straps attached to the bottom of the knapsack with wooden toggles.

(Left) Unit details marked on the campaign cover of a cartridge box.

(Left & above) In 1809 ten companies of military *infirmiers* were formed - one per Army Corps - to collect the wounded on the battlefield and to work in hospitals. Each company of 108 men was led by a *centenier* (ranked as a second lieutenant) and a *sous-centenier*. From 1813 their muskets were recalled, and they were equipped as *brancardiers* - stretcher bearers. They worked in pairs; each man of a pair carried one pole and one wooden stretcher endpiece. A simple inverted U-shape painted white, with *"SECURS AUX BRAVES"* in red on the horizontal bar, this could be strapped to his pack when not in use. A sash-like waistband was fitted with pockets for dressings, etc.

The infantry-style uniform was chestnut brown faced with red; this corporal has the uniform and shako plate of the 1812 regulations, the latter bearing his company number; the turn-back emblem was a brown star.

The sooner a wounded man could be treated the greater his chances of recovery; but there were never nearly enough infirmiers or surgeons to cope with the numbers of casualties in major actions. It was not always easy to persuade stretcher-bearers to venture into the middle of a continuing battle, and their function - taking them from under the immediate eyes of authority - gave them opportunities to go to ground.

The most famous of French army surgeons was Baron Dominique Jean Larrey, Surgeon-General to the Imperial Guard and, from

1812, to the Grande Armée. Although his first responsibility was to the Guard, this élite rarely saw action until the later Empire, so the limited resources of his great humanitarian were sometimes available to the Line. Larrey introduced the "Flying Ambulance", an innovative vehicle superior to the more cumbersome "Wurst" of Surgeon-in-Chief Pierre Francois Percy; but there were always pitifully few of these available.

Right) A surgeon examines something unpleasant after an amputation. . .From 1806 the staff element of each fighting regiment was to include a surgeon-major and four assistant surgeons. Official uniform was a single-breasted tail coat in *bleu barbeau,* a lighter shade than that worn by the infantry, faced crimson at collar and cuffs, which bore varying numbers of gold lace loops. On field service, however, many wore either simple dark blue surtouts or some version of regimental dress. Surgeons wore red waistcoats, physicians black. Shot, shell and blade produced massive wounds, fatal penetration of major

organs, and traumatic amputation. Gangrene and general septicaemia were also great killers, given the state of medical ignorance; dirty fragments of cloth and other debris were often carried into wounds. Amputations were standard procedure for all serious limb wounds; in the absence of anaesthetic post-operative shock killed many patients. Large numbers of men crammed together under rudimentary conditions of hygiene also routinely fell victim to the silent killers - dysentery, cholera, typhus and typhoid carried off many more soldiers than ever fell in battle.

(Below) The kind of implements used by a period surgeon. Bones shattered by shot needed rounding off with a bone chisel or amputation with a bone saw. The low-velocity musket balls often lodged in the wounds, and had to be located with various probes and removed with forceps. French practice was to create a flap of skin when amputating a limb, to fold neatly over the stump and help close the wound as it healed. Maggots bound into wounds obligingly ate only dead flesh, thus cleaning them efficiently.

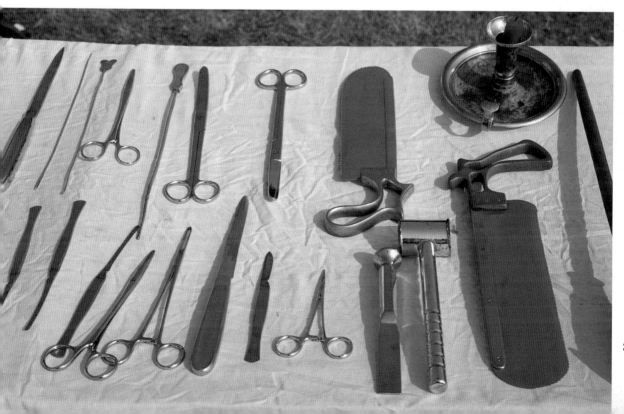

A *sapeur* of the 18e de Ligne. These pioneers, chosen from the best and strongest men of the grenadier company, carried out field engineering duties - e.g. clearing paths and camp grounds, building barricades, loop-holing walls, etc. - as well as taking the van in assaults on enemy field fortifications. The courage and strength demanded of them were marked by their place on the march, at the head of the battalion with the Eagle and band; by their privileged duty as HQ guards; and by distinctive uniform features. They were always bearded; they wore fur bonnets with grenadier plumes (and sometimes brass plates,

hough not in the 18th Line),
nd leather aprons. As well as
nuskets or carbines,
ccording to availability, they
arried felling axes in leather
ases, and special rooster-
eaded sabres; and their
rossbelts were handsomely
adged.

Perhaps the most famous
se of the felling axe was by
ne giant Lt.Legros of the 2e
éger at Waterloo. Seizing
ne from a pioneer, Legros
ved up to his nickname
L'Enfonceur, "The Smasher")
y breaking through the rear
ate of Hougoumont château
nd leading his men into the
ourtyard. In desperate hand-
o-hand fighting all except the
rummer boy were killed by
ne British garrison of 3rd
oot Guards (but not before a
ioneer had cut clean off the
and of the Hanoverian
t.Wilder in the mêlée.)

This re-enactor, Robert
eyne, is a metal worker by
ade; he made his own axe
nd crossbelt badges – note
ne pioneer's crossed axes,
ne grenadier grenade, and
on-masks.

GRENADIERS

(Right) A grenadier of the Revolutionary Wars at the Jena re-enactment. Initially the idea of distinguishing one company in each battalion as an élite was unpopular, given the egalitarian ideals of the Revolution: Thiebault tells us that the first proposals to introduce such companies in the National Guard were badly received. Although the amalgamated Demi-Brigades de Bataille of 1793-94 included grenadiers (as did the light infantry Chasseur battalions at least by 1792, under the name of carabiniers), the red fringed epaulettes which should have been their exclusive distinction seem also to have been worn fairly promiscuously by fusiliers.

(Opposite, top left) Grenadier wearing the uniform of c.1805, with the red wool epaulettes and red-plumed bicorn of his company; grenadiers were to be at least 1.75m (5ft 9in) tall. This stalwart was photographed at Jena enjoying excellent German wine. Gen. Desaix, the hero of Marengo, liked to tell the story of a grenadier who - having drunk too much wine, and too indiscriminately - was observed wandering around muttering:"Red and white, red and white - if you can't agree with one another, out you both go!"

(Opposite, top right) Grenadier in the field, c.1805. In October 1801 an order confirmed the use of the tall fur bonnet on parade and in battle. Officially of bearskin, it was often made of goatskin in practice. It had a top rear patch in red cloth with a white braid cross or red and blue quarters (the so-called"monkey's backside"); and a brass front plate usually embossed with this flaming grenade badge. The tassel was a fixture; a plume and cord festoons were added for parades.

(Right) Off duty the grenadier's headgear was the usual *bonnet de police à la dragonne* worn by French soldiers of all arms of service since the 1780s, with a red grenade badge on the front of the "turban".

(Opposite) Outside the village of Cospeda on the field of Jena, reconstructed grenadiers of several periods of the NapoleonicWars load their muskets. Note the grenade turn-back emblems.

41

(**Right & below**) Grenadiers and Eagle of the recreated 111th Line. They wear the new shako of the 1812 regulations, perhaps occasioned by shortage and expense of bearskin due to the Royal Navy's blockade. Slightly taller than the fusilier type, with red top and bottom bands and side chevrons, it could be embellished for formal dress with a red plume or pompon and red cords. The coats are of pre-1812 cut, and the shako plate is the 1810 pattern - a positively conservative departure from regulations, considering the many contemporary descriptions of regimental peculiarities.

(**Left & below**) Even if the Bardin regulations of 1812 were supposed to bring about practical and economical simplifications of the uniform, the grenadier shako - when fully furnished - is still splendidly impressive. The 1812 pattern shako plate, in the shape of the Imperial eagle over a crescent-shaped Amazon shield, is pierced here with the number of the 55th Line flanking an embossed grenade. This soldier was photographed during the June 1995 Waterloo commemoration, when rain and mud played their part in ensuring historical authenticity.

(**Below**) Full unit details painted on the grenadier's pouch flap cover.

(**Above & right**) On the field of Jena, October 1996: the French line advance, and an opportunistic grenadier NCO pauses for a moment to loot the pack of a fallen King's German Legion rifleman. Even on warm days some soldiers used to retain the grey/brown greatcoat: it offered some slight protection against cuts and stabs.

(Top & above)
Virtually every account of
Napoleonic warfare mentions
the blinding effect of the
thick powder smoke which
hung over the firing line
after a few volleys, unless
there was a brisk wind. This
single volley on a heavy,
damp day at Jena provides
confirmation, though still
only a feeble imitation
of what a three-deep battle
line in close order,
thousands strong, must
have produced at a
rate of two or three
rounds per minute.

45

VOLTIGEURS

Although some regiments of the Line had in practice anticipated the reform by several years, it was in September 1804 that each battalion was officially ordered to form a second élite company - of light skirmishers or voltigeurs - by transforming one of the fusilier companies. By 1808 the normal battalion establishment was one grenadier, one voltigeur and four fusilier companies.

Voltigeurs were supposed to be a maximum of 1.6m (5ft 3in) tall, their officers an inch taller, though this was not strictly enforced. At first their only uniform distinctions were a buff (chamois) collar, soon changed to bright yellow, and a buglehorn turn-back and fatigue cap emblem. However, as élite troops they tended to affect sabres, green and yellow epaulettes, plumes and sabre knots, and moustaches. There was a good deal of variation in detail from regiment to regiment.

(Right) This voltigeur was seen at 6am on a dewy morning on the field of Austerlitz in 1995.

(Below) The cap, collar and epaulette detail, the latter in green with yellow crescents.

(Below right) Sergeant of voltigeurs preparing for battle at Vauchamps; one indication of rank is the more elaborate epaulette with gold threads mixed into the green fringe, and a yellow edging to the strap.

46

(**Left**) Sergeant of voltigeurs of the 96th Line on the field of Jena. A confirmed regimental peculiarity was the cuff flap in the same red-piped yellow as the collar, instead of the usual blue. He has turned his bicorn "fore-and-aft" so as not to knock it off while handling his musket. Officially, when the whole battalion was drawn up the grenadier company was positioned at the right of the line, the voltigeur company at the left.

(**Below**) Note that the sergeant has a wooden canteen, and the grenadier behind him a natural gourd. Water bottles were not an issue item, and each soldier had to shift for himself to procure some sort of flask. Death from thirst and heat during summer campaigns was not unusual; on the advance into Russia in 1812 we read of desperate men drinking from puddles of horses' urine or sucking liquid mud. Marshal Davout was one commander who made a point of ensuring that his men had some sort of canteen whenever he could.

(Right) Voltigeur sergeant, here wearing loose white campaign trousers over or instead of his breeches and gaiters, loading his musket in the kneeling position. This is easy enough when widely spaced out in a skirmish line, but would be a good deal more awkward when packed into the usual close ranks. Voltigeurs were taught to work in pairs, one man covering while the other loaded, and resisting the temptation to both fire at once.

(Left) The main charge ignites, while the smoke of the priming still hangs around the sergeant's face. To those used to firing modern weapons the pause or "hang-fire" between pulling the trigger of a flintlock and the detonation of the main charge is quite noticeable; to keep a steady aim through this - and despite the flare of the priming close in front of the face - takes practice.

When firing in massed formation individual marksmanship was not a realistic factor: the officers "fired" their companies and battalions like a single giant shotgun at equally massed targets. However, the skirmishers sent out between the lines to harass or provoke the enemy, or to thin their advancing ranks before the main contact, did pick off individual targets. We read of voltigeurs sniping at officers and artillery crews in particular.

(Above) Voltigeur of the 45th Line taking aim. Green epaulettes with red crescents were quite a common variation. The shako and plate are of 1806 pattern.

(Right) The Bardin regulations of 1812 gave voltigeurs the same shako decorations as the grenadiers but with yellow lace instead of red. Epaulettes were yellow, but there are many examples of variations such as yellow straps and fringes with green crescents, or vice versa.

(**Left**) The colonel's 1812 pattern shako plate has the regimental number of the 21e de Ligne cut out; the officer's usual gold lace top band and bullion cord festoon; protective chinscales; and one of a wide range of recorded discs, tufts and pompons. His gorget has the eagle in silver on a gilt plate. The sword is a slim, straight-bladed épee with a single bar guard; curved sabres were often preferred by officers of the élite companies.

OFFICERS

Each of a Line regiment's (usually) four *bataillons de guerre* was commanded by a *chef de bataillon* (equivalent to lieutenant-colonel). Each of the six companies was commanded by a *capitaine* assisted by one *lieutenant* and one *sous-lieutenant*. The regimental staff included the *colonel,* a major, four *chefs de bataillon,* five adjutants and five assistants, together with various senior NCOs and specialists.

(**Right**) On campaign infantry officers rode to war (when they could), although company officers led their men into action on foot. Their full dress uniform was expensive and easily soiled, so normal campaign dress was often this simple dark blue coat - surtout - without the white reversed lapels. This officer is identified as a colonel by his pair of gold bullion fringed epaulettes. The major wore the same but with silver straps; the chef de bataillon, gold, but with a fringe on the left shoulder only.

50

(Above & above right)
Senior officers of the
Emperor's army might
acquire riches, and might
display them by the quality of
their uniforms and
accoutrements. However, the
great majority of the
regimental infantry officers
were of quite humble
background and had to live
on their pay. Many found this
hard; despite the Revolution
the expectation that an
officer should live in a
gentlemanly style had not
entirely disappeared.

The rank of this captain of
the 18th Line (recreated here
by a German group at the Jena
re-enactment) is identified by
his epaulettes: gold, with a
fringe on the left shoulder
only. His 1806 shako bears an
added disc displaying the
number of the 2nd Company.

(Right) Senior staff officers
- *Adjutants-Commandants* -
belonged to a distinct corps
dating back to 1790. One was
assigned to each division and
corps of the army on campaign
as chief-of-staff; they
supervised such matters as the
daily plan of march, camping,
billeting and provisions. This
officer wears a double-
breasted riding overcoat -
redingote - with the gold lace
loops of his appointment at
collar and cuff. His epaulettes
mark his rank as the equivalent
of colonel. A folding telescope
would have been part of every
conscientious officer's
campaign kit.

(Left & below) The higher in rank an officer rose, the more gold embroidery he displayed. While not perfectly accurate in detail, this re-enactor's coat gives a reasonable impression of the proportion of a marshal's surface which was encrusted with bullion!

(Right) Senior officers climb the Landgrafenberg hill at Jena towards the battlefield on the heights.

(Left & below) The French army employed civilians on the Intendant-General's staff; these commissariat officials served on all staffs down to division, and on those of fortress garrisons. The rank of these senior *commissaire-ordonnateurs* was indicated by the degree of silver embroidery on collar and cuffs.

(Right) Being civilians, the commissariat staff enjoyed a good deal of leeway when purchasing their uniforms. Brighter coloured cloth and finer materials were deliberately flaunted by those who could afford them, and a theatrical tendency was noted in the outfits of many non-combatant specialists and officials.

(Left) Staff officers chat in the grounds of the Château de Montmirail during the re-enactment of the 1814 French campaign.

(Below left) The imposing colonel of the 21st Line, in 1812 regulation shako and *habit-veste*. The 21st were one of Napoleon's most distinguished regiments; they fought at Austerlitz, Jena, Eylau, Eckmühl, Wagram, Saragossa, Smolensk, Borodino, Dresden, and with I Corps in the 1815 Waterloo campaign.

(Below) Epaulette detail, company officer; like captains, lieutenants wore a gold fringed epaulette on the left shoulder and an unfringed contre-epaulette on the right, the senior grade with one red stripe on the strap and the junior with two.

(Right) Many messengers were needed at every level of command, from the staff of a *général de brigade* to that of the Emperor himself. These *aides-de-camp* wore the fashionable dress of the hussar regiments, and some marshals tended to put their own aides into showy uniforms of their own design. (Murat, predictably, was one of these, his aides being bedecked in *amarante* and *chamois*!) In 1807 Napoleon attempted to regulate the situation, ordering marshals' aides into a dark blue hussar-style uniform with scarlet trim; but marshals who had been granted the title of Prince continued to choose uniforms to personal taste. This splendid aide, wearing a late Empire hussar uniform, was photographed at the Château de la Gataudière, family home of Prince Murat de Chasseloup-Laubat, during the "Bivouac Napoleon" held there in June 1996.

(**Above**) The 21e de Ligne drawn up prior to a revue. This group are the largest in the British Napoleonic Association; they were presented with their Eagle by the present-day 21e Régiment, whom they visit bi-annually, and enjoy official recognition from the French Army.

(**Right**) Sergeant drummer of the 21st Line wearing the dark green coatee with yellow and green lace decreed as the universal uniform for drummers and trumpeters in 1812; before that date they wore a variety of uniforms according to the commander's whim and pocket, traditionally in reversed colours, e.g. red faced with blue. This was not mere vanity and show; the company's two drummers passed the officers' commands in the deafening noise of battle by a series of rolls and beats which the troops had been taught to recognize, and they had to be instantly visible when an officer looked around for them. Note the brass drum; the Emperor declared that it made his favourite music, because it sounded like the roar of artillery.

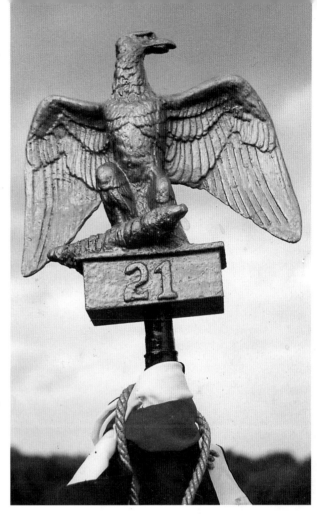

(Above left & above)
The Eagle-bearer of the 21st Line (in this case the Adjutant of the re-enactment group, Chris Durkin); and the bronze Eagle itself. These famous standards, presented by Napoleon in person, were always more important than the flags attached to their shafts. Although irreverent soldiers sometimes called them "cuckoos", they embodied the spirit of the regiment, and many soldiers were inspired to fight and die under their wings. The sculptor Chaudet was commissioned to produce the original pattern in 1804, taking as his model the eagles of Imperial Rome. They were constructed in six parts and mounted on a hollow section plinth, which with the eagle itself measured about 31cm (12.2in) in height with a maximum wing span of 25.5cm (10in); weighing 1.85kg (nearly 4lbs), they were mounted on a blue shaft around 2m long.

(Left) The colour party, selected from fusiliers, were officially appointed only with the approval of Napoleon himself. The *porte-aigle* had to be a junior officer of at least ten years' service and (at least under the early Empire) had to have fought at Ulm, Austerlitz, Jena and Friedland. He was escorted by "second and third bearers", who ranked as sergeants but were paid as sergeant-majors - this was one way of rewarding brave veterans who could not aspire to that rank by reason of illiteracy. Their uniforms varied but were always splendid, including bearskins or, from 1809, this version of the crested brass helmet of the Carabinier heavy cavalry. They carried halberds with long pennons, red for the *deuxiéme* and white for the *troisiéme;* when waved, these would supposedly spook the horses of attacking cavalry. They were also armed with a sabre and pistols.

57

(**Right & below**) The 21st Line in action at Jena, October 1996, wearing 1812 uniform with loose white campaign trousers. These trousers were made up at unit level from any available cloth or looted from captured enemy stores, and were often seen in dark blue, brown or grey. In a period when some latitude was normal even in a unit's full dress uniform, such campaign items were considered more a matter for pragmatism than for strict regulation.

Note the crowned N cypher in gold on the turn-backs of the fusilier officer's short-tailed coatee; and the brown leather campaign haversack - typical of the sort of field equipment a junior officer might buy for himself.

(Left & above) A long-serving fusilier sergeant of the 21st showing off the 1812 regulation uniform and shako, with campaign trousers and the sabre-briquet of his rank. The facings of his habit-veste are convincingly faded with use. The fusilier shako was dressed with white cords for full dress; the pompon was in company colour. The sequence was supposedly green, light blue, orange and violet for the 1st to 4th Companies of the 1st Battalion, the corresponding companies of the other battalions bearing the company number in black on a white disc fringed with wool in these colours.

(**Right & below**) A company of the 21st advance in line on the field of Jena; halt, present, and prepare to fire. The ranges at which opposing battle lines traded fire could be lower than 50 yards, and the casualties could literally pile up on the same spot after a number of volleys. Lejeune describes the very wide main street of Sokolnitz "entirely covered with the dead and wounded of both sides. The corpses were heaped up on one another, and it was almost impossible to ride across the tangle of weapons and broken human bodies."

Experienced commanders knew that when a regiment's nerve broke it was no good trying to control them until they had recovered. Gen. Comte de Ségur describes the 4th Line breaking before the Russian Horse Guards at Austerlitz: "covered with blood, and having lost their Eagle and the greater part of their arms" they ran away past Napoleon's staff, "distracted by fear...In reply to our reproaches...they shouted mechanically '*Vive l'Empereur!*', while fleeing faster than ever." Napoleon gave a pitying smile, and gestured "Let them go".

(**Right**) Fire and movement; the 21st open fire, while Light Infantry skirmish forward on the flank.

The officer who became too upset about casualties had no place in Napoleon's army. Ségur expressed his concern to Gen. Vandamme at Austerlitz when he realised that some 150 men passing them were all who survived from one of Vandamme's battalions. "Yes, indeed", replied the general; "it is impossible to make a good omelette without breaking a great many eggs."

IN CAMP

A camp ground with neatly piled arms and equipment. During a campaign of movement camps were much more makeshift than this. "When it was cold everyone slept around their campfires, but that broiled you on one side while you froze on the other. You could keep turning over, like Saint Lawrence (martyred on a spit), but that was not at all convenient....Reveille is never amusing; you have slept, because you were exhausted, but when you get up your limbs are numb, and moustaches look like tufts of alfalfa, with dewdrops on every hair. Your teeth are clenched, and you have to really rub your gums to restore circulation."

Each squad - a quarter of a company, and thus anything between 15 and 30 men, under a corporal - formed a mess (*ordinaire*). The mess equipment - a 5 1/2 litre *bidon*, a camp kettle, assorted messtins, a hatchet for cutting firewood, etc. - was divided up between the squad, who took turns to carry it. Soldiers throughout history have not always been prudent campaigners, and in good times they tend to "lose" things rather than carry them, trusting to luck or larceny to replace them. Although men of the Grande Armée certainly ate raw horsemeat (and worse) when desperate with hunger, a man with a cookpot could usually trade its loan for a place at the fire and a share of the food cooked in it.

Napoleon's great weakness as a commander was his failure to make adequate provision for feeding his men. The French army relied to an unrealistic extent on "living off the country" - i.e., on plundering the wretched peasants over whose lands they marched - and on the hope of capturing enemy stores. As a result, the troops were nearly always hungry once they had made a few marches beyond reach of their depots; and if they were still in the field in late autumn or winter they weakened, slowed, sickened, and eventually starved.

(Above) Corporal of the 21st Line wearing the sleeved waistcoat of the 1812 regulations, with its blue collar, cuffs and shoulder straps; and the new fatigue cap of that year, the *pokalem,* which had folding ear/neck flaps. Men often marched wearing the greatcoat directly over the waistcoat, but usually wore their uniform coat for battle (if they had one - the teenage conscripts of 1813-14 often received only partial clothing issue).

(Above right) Living in the field means constant small repairs to clothing and kit. This soldier enlists the help of a *cantiniére* or *vivandiére* to sew up his shako.

(Right) A soldier of the 18th Line with his family.

(Left) A little opportunist looting by a *vivandiére* after an action. These women - who accompanied the regiment on campaign with semi-official status, and made a living selling the men alcohol, tobacco and other comforts - were not known for being squeamish. They shared all the hardship of the march and the dangers of campaign, providing for themselves and for their menfolk; some were married to a succession of NCOs, marrying another without delay if his predecessor was killed. Period drawings sometimes show them wearing jaunty modifications of military jackets.

Rignt) The *vivandiére's* randy keg, patriotically ecorated, and metal cups.

(Right) Supper is served - rather more lavishly than would have been usual in our period, unless the squad had the luck to be the first to spot some unfortunate peasant's pigsty. In France all bachelors between 20 and 25 were liable for military service under the early Empire (the age limit dropped later); so it is not surprising that marriages increased by 50% between 1805 and 1809. Even so, every marching army had a "tail" of camp followers, and some hardy women managed to accompany their husbands or sweethearts on campaign, even with small children. Many a soldier left wounded on the field owed his life to his woman's courage in coming searching for him.

(Left) In the early days, before shorter styles became the fashion, a soldier needed the help of a comrade to dress his queue and cadenettes. Often a unit had its own self-taught experts, who earned a few extra pennies drinking money by this service. The same was true of many skills which the soldiers needed but which Napoleonic armies did not provide, such as shoe repairs, simple tailoring, rudimentary metalwork - even folk-medecine. Conscripts came from every walk of life, in a period when hand crafts provided most manufactured goods; in the average battalion there must have been at least one man who could turn his hand to almost any trade if it was made worth his while.

NAPOLEON'S ALLIED TROOPS:

SAXONY

Napoleon's campaigns demanded far more troops than France alone could provide; and he often pressed defeated nations who had submitted to French satellite status to provide him with cannon-fodder. For his invasion of Russia in June 1812 he amassed an army of more than 450,000 men of whom less than 200,000 were French, the remainder being provided by Austria, Prussia and other German states, Poland, Italy, even Portugal.

In the Jena-Auerstädt campaign of 1806 the Saxons fought against the French as allies of Prussia. The speed with which Napoleon defeated the highly respected Prussian army stunned Europe; but one aspect of the rout caught Napoleon's attention - the stubborn rearguard action fought by the Saxon army. As an ally of France one of Saxony's obligations thereafter was to provide the Grande Armée with up to 20,000 men when required.

Saxon troops fought against Prussia and Russia in 1807; against Austria in 1809; and in Russia and Germany in 1812-13.

(Below) Desertion was not uncommon; most recaptured deserters were returned to the ranks, sometimes in penal battalions, but occasionally examples had to be made. Note the sergeant's ornate spontoon or half-pike, and his white hat cockade.

(Below) This is the uniform worn by Saxon infantry before reforms along French lines in 1810. The white woollen coat has long tails and is cut high at the front, exposing the white waistcoat. These men wear the blue facings of the Regiment "von Bevilaqua", which fought in the 1st Division of Lefebvre's Corps in the 1807 Friedland campaign. The red stock was worn by all units. Equipment comprises a cartridge box on a single broad crossbelt, a sabre frogged to a waistbelt, and a small calfskin knapsack slung across the back.

(Left) The sergeant of Saxon musketeers carried a spontoon instead of a musket (until 1809); as in most period armies, it was more a visible staff of office and an aid to pushing his men into straight ranks than a practical weapon. His hat brim is edged with scallopped braid; he shows shirt frills at neck and cuff; and (like corporals, who carried a halberd-headed polearm) he has a long cane looped to a coat button. This was used for inflicting summary punishment; in battle it was passed under the arm and slipped under the fastening of the coat tail turn-backs to hold it out of the way. The pocket watch would be a rarity for an NCO; perhaps it was taken from a fallen officer on the battlefield, and sold to the sergeant cheaply for drinking money by one of his men?

(Left) The small bicorn has d and white tufts - in fact, e tassels at the ends of the t brim adjustment cord; ese were worn throughout e army. The pompon at the ft front was in white and the gimental facing colour.

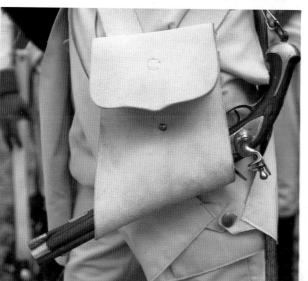

(Left) The unusual leather pistol holster and clip arrangement worn on the crossbelt by Saxon sergeants and corporals.

(Right) When on campaign the Saxon army were burdened and slowed by the heavy baggage train typical of the 18th century. Encampments were set up according to strict regulations, each tent in its place. This tent - for the storage of muskets - is reconstructed to period specifications, and the required sentry is posted outside it.

(Left) An off-duty soldier wearing a simple forage cap with band in his regimental colour, smoking a clay pipe. (On being asked if all he did was drink and smoke, one veteran replied, "No - sometimes I smoke and *then* I drink.") Given his negligible pay and restricted daily life, smoking and drinking were more or less the limit of the common soldier's available pleasures..

(Right) . . .Though some days were doubtless better than others. Note the calfskin pack slung on a diagonal strap; and the set-back position of the coat shoulder strap.

(Below) The Saxon undress cap, worn by a grenadier standing in line for his rations - note the wooden spoon thrust under his belt.

(Above) A complete re-organisation of the Saxon army along French lines began in 1810. Conscription replaced voluntary enlistment; the regiments were organised in permanent brigades and divisions; and each regiment would henceforward have two battalions each of two grenadier and eight musketeer companies. The grenadier companies of each brigade were assembled in a single battalion.

The uniform remained white with coloured regimental facings, but was recut in the French style, and a shako replaced the bicorn. These grenadiers are identified by their red shako pompons; officially they should also be wearing red fringed epaulettes, but these were often absent. The fanion identifies the Grenadier-Bataillon "von Liebenau", formed from the grenadier companies of the regiments "Prinz Friedrich" and "Prinz Clemens", which fought in the 21st Division, VII Corps of the Grande Armée in Russia. Note the drab cloth shako cover at right, fastened with wooden toggles.

(**above & right**) Prior to 1792 the Saxon army were almost devoid of light infantry, a Schützen element integral to the Line regiments being formed in 1793. These sharpshooters were sent into action with the order "Ausschwarmen", upon which they left the ranks and deployed. In 1802 the Schützen were gathered together into two separate light infantry battalions, although they were not tactically employed as such until 1806. An order of May 1808 removed them officially from the Line battalions and formed regular Schützen battalions each of four companies. Two - "von Metzsch" and "von Egidy" - fought at Wagram in 1809. From May 1810 each was expanded to regimental size, the 1st redesignated "Le Coq" and the 2nd as "von Sahr", with paper strengths of 1,625 men. His uniform cut to the same pattern as the Line infantry but in dark green, this post-1810 private of Schützen has black facings with red trim. Prior to 1810 the only light infantry distinction had been a 12in/14in green plume, the uniforms being the same as those of their parent Line units.

(**Above left & left**) Wearing the 1810 French-style uniform, grenadiers of the Saxon Line Regiment "Prinz Maximilian", which served in the 24th Division, VII Corps of the Grande Armée in the 1813 campaign. Note grenade badge on cartridge box flaps.

(**Above & right**) Distinctive in their red coats with yellow cuffs, lapels and collars, men of the Saxon Leib-Grenadier-Garde. This unit served in the 1st Division of Bernadotte's IX Corps in 1809; and alongside the "Prinz Maximilian" in the 24th Division, VII Corps in 1813.

ITALY

The political history of the several states making up the Italian peninsula and Sicily in Napoleonic times was extremely complex. Suffice it to say here that at various dates both the northern Kingdom of Italy and the southern Kingdom of the Two Sicilies (Naples) fell under Napoleon's sway, and contributed troops to his armies. The Italians sent several regiments to the 1806 campaign against Prussia; fought Austria in the Alps in 1809; and contributed six infantry and three cavalry units to IV Corps of the Grande Armée in Russia, fighting at Smolensk and Borodino - of some 20,000 men, perhaps 14,000 perished. The survivors were reinforced for the 1813 German campaign; and seven infantry regiments, two of cavalry and plentiful artillery also served in Spain between 1808 and 1813.

(Left, top & above) The infantry units sent to Spain were the 4th to 8th Line regiments, each of four battalions, each battalion of one grenadier, one voltigeur and four fusilier companies on the French pattern. This is a sergeant of voltigeurs of the 5th Line, wearing the white uniform of French cut issued after 1806; before that date the Italian infantry had been dressed in green faced with red. Note the yellow collar piped green, mixed green and silver cords and epaulettes of company and rank, and company turn-back badges. All smallclothes and equipment were of French type, though this NCO in the heat of Spain wears lightweight ticking trousers.

(Above, top & right)
A grenadier of the Italian 5th Line; compare his collar with that of the voltigeur. His shako is dressed with grenadier red cords and plume; epaulettes are French in style; turn-backs and shako chinscale bosses bear the grenade emblem. The white, red and green national cockade is based upon the Italian flag designed by Napoleon.

POLAND

Poland, historically doomed to be crushed between neighbouring powers, was partitioned between Russia, Prussia and Austria in 1795. Many Polish exiles fled to France, forming units for service in her armies in Italy and in the Rhineland. They hoped that Revolutionary France would free their homeland; but when Napoleon crushed their occupiers in 1807 he only sponsored the creation of a rump state under the title "Grand Duchy of Warsaw".

Although this fell far short of the hopes of Polish patriots many tens of thousands of Poles would serve on in his armies, earning a glowing reputation for dash and courage on battlefields from Spain to Moscow. In Russia Polish units made up the entire V Corps of the Grande Armée, and its VIII Corps in 1813; they were led by the fearless Prince Poniatowski, who died in battle, a Marshal of the Empire, in October 1813. In Spain the infantry of the Vistula Legion were among the most reliable regiments in the French forces.

(Above) Polish grenadier corporal on the field of Jena. The corporal's rank is marked by two yellow stripes above the cuffs, and a yellow braid edging to the headgear.

(Left) From left to right: a corporal of grenadiers, a grenadier, a fusilier and two voltigeurs of Polish infantry in post-1810 uniform, complete with the traditional *czapka* square-topped headgear.

(Right) Polish fusilier charging through the mud of the Jena battlefield. The Pole distinguished themselves in Russia, but at great cost: of some 30,000 men with the colours in late June 1812, les than 3,000 survived to reach Warsaw that November - bu they still had their Eagles, ar 40 cannon.

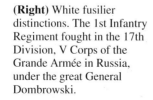

(Left) Typical voltigeur distinctions on collar, epaulettes and headgear. Each regiment had three battalions of one grenadier, one voltigeur and four fusilier companies.

(Right) White fusilier distinctions. The 1st Infantry Regiment fought in the 17th Division, V Corps of the Grande Armée in Russia, under the great General Dombrowski.

ARTILLERY

Napoleon always said that "It is with artillery that one makes war"- hardly a surprising opinion considering his own early service in that branch. He always remained interested in its development, and it was said that the Emperor was capable of taking his place in a gun crew until the end of his career.

Napoleonic artillery was divided between Foot and Horse units; both types were, of course, moved by teams of draught horses (six to 12 per gun), but in the former the men marched, and in the latter they were mounted either on horses or on the limbers and ammunition caissons. This allowed Horse Artillery - in theory - to keep up with the cavalry on the march, and to move quickly around the battlefield; the Foot Artillery, once emplaced, needed much longer to change position or get on the road.

France led the world in the standardisation of guns, calibres and equipment. From 1776 the brilliant Inspector-General of Artillery, Jean Baptiste de Gribeauval, had supervised the introduction of a greatly improved and much lighter range of unified designs - guns, carriages, limbers, ammunition wagons, mobile forges and other specialised equipment - with standard tools and accessories. This had the great advantage of making many items interchangeable for field repairs and maintenance, which was innovative for its period.

Guns were classified by the weight of their shot. The field artillery consisted mostly of 6-pounder, 8-pdr. and 12-pdr. cannon (long-barrelled pieces which fired at a fairly flat trajectory out to the longest attainable ranges); and, in smaller numbers, 6in-calibre howitzers (short-barrelled pieces which lobbed projectiles at a high angle and relatively shorter range, to drop on targets behind cover). In 1810 there were nine administrative regiments of Foot Artillery, each with about 22 tactical companies (batteries); company composition varied, but a normal strength under the early Empire was six 8-pdrs. and two howitzers, with 12-pdrs. steadily replacing the 8-pdrs. as the years passed.

The standard proportion for artillery in a campaign army was one Foot and one Horse company per infantry division and one Horse battery per cavalry division. Napoleon also built up an artillery reserve for massed fire; and for some campaigns lighter 3-pdr. and 4-pdr. guns were additionally allocated directly to infantry regiments. Napoleon aimed to provide his troops with artillery support at a ratio of 5 guns per 1,000 men, but only achieved about 3.5 per 1,000.

(**Below**) Foot Artillery with a small-calibre gun on the field of Jena, October 1996. Serving a cannon is very thirsty work.

(Right & below) Crews serving their guns at Jena in the pre-1807 uniforms of the Line and Guard Foot Artillery.

(Rignt) Fuzes used in artillery re-enactment, with a Y-shaped end to catch the flame quickly. They are inserted into the touchhole of the cannon, the end penetrating the powder charge. Period fuzes were made of either quill or tubes of copper, filled with fine gunpowder and capped with flannel steeped in an inflammable mixture.

(Bottom right) Two essential artillery tools, always kept with the gun: the sponge end of the rammer staff, soaked in water and used to swab out the barrel after each shot; and the wormscrew, to scour any large cartridge debris out of the barrel.

(**Right**) The uniform of the Artillerie à Pied de Ligne, c.1805. The Foot Artillery wore infantry-style uniforms in dark blue faced and trimmed with scarlet. The collar was blue, usually piped red; the cuffs and cuff-flaps red, or blue piped red, the one usually contrasting with the other; the lapels and pockets blue piped red; the turnbacks solid red with blue "grenade" ornaments. For service or winter dress black gaiters were worn, white for full dress or summer service. From about 1808 the dark blue breeches were increasingly covered on campaign by looser blue trousers, which by 1813 often bore red stripes down the outside seam. Waistcoats were usually dark blue, though sometimes red, and buttons brass. The bicorn was replaced from 1807 by a shako. The shorter habit-veste replaced the longer-tailed coat from 1812.

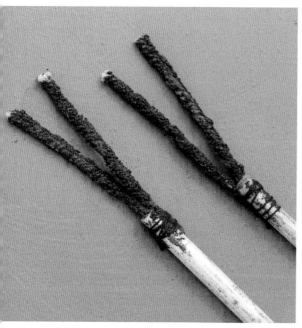

81

HORSE ARTILLERY

Although the French army had experimented with horse artillery in the late 1770s, it was not until 1792 that the first companies appeared with the full complement of gunners mounted rather than riding on the caissons; and throughout the Napoleonic Wars there was always a shortage of horses. (One teething problem was inevitable given the origins of the personnel: the gunnery instructors came from the Foot Artillery and the rankers from Line Infantry grenadier companies, which did much for their strength and aggression but little for their equestrian skills.) The size of the arm varied; but in 1801-13 there were usually six Horse Artillery regiments, each of three squadrons, each of two companies, each of four 6-pdr.guns and two howitzers.

*   *   *

One of the most famous and most innovative uses of artillery was at the battle of Friedland in 1807. The artillery commander of Victor's Corps, Sénarmont, obtained permission from Victor to mass all the artillery of the three divisions (totalling 38 pieces). He divided them into a reserve of 8 guns and two artillery groups each of 10 x 6-pdrs., 2 x 4-pdrs. and 3 howitzers. The reserve was kept out of sight of the enemy behind the left hand battery; the two artillery groups were deployed forward, opening fire at a range of 400 metres.

After firing five or six rounds the groups advanced alternately to a range of about 200m, closely protected by an infantry battalion and four dragoon regiments. Another 20 rounds of roundshot were pumped into the Russian lines; then Sénarmont decided to force the issue and prolonged his batteries at ranges of only about 60 metres from the enemy battle line. From here they could shower the Russians with canister shot, breaking their infantry and routing the supporting Russian artillery. A Russian cavalry charge was disrupted by their own fleeing troops, then broken up with canister.

French infantry now moved up to occupy the ground the Russians had vacated, and indeed reached the town of Friedland itself, still supported by Sénarmont's batteries. His losses were relatively light considering the results he had achieved : 66 dead and wounded men, and 53 horses. Sénarmont would repeat these offensive artillery tactics in the Peninsula, at Ocana and Medellin - both times against the Spanish, and both times successfully.

(Below) A mobile field forge essential to any period army and particularly to the artillery. It was not only a question of keeping large numbers of horses shod; the guns and their accessories represented a wide range of specialist iron fittings which saw hard daily use and needed constant repair and maintenance.

(Above) Horse gunners, one wearing the dark blue and red *bonnet de police* and red-frogged blue dolman jacket of that branch, waiting to go into action. In reality it would be rare to see the round of "fixed" ammunition usually resting on the gun - for safety reasons all powder charges had to be kept covered and enclosed until the moment of use.

(Right) Reconstruction of a Gribeauval cast bronze field gun; wheel diameter was 152cm (60in). The sponge bucket is slung underneath and the tools and handspikes are fitted in brackets along the sides of the carriage. The chest carried between the cheeks of the trail held 9 to 15 rounds of ammunition for immediate use; the accompanying caisson (ammunition wagon) carried another 48 to 62, depending on calibre. Napoleon said that he liked his artillery to carry enough ammunition for "two good battles".

(Top right) The wooden tompion which kept dirt and rain out of the barrel when not in use.

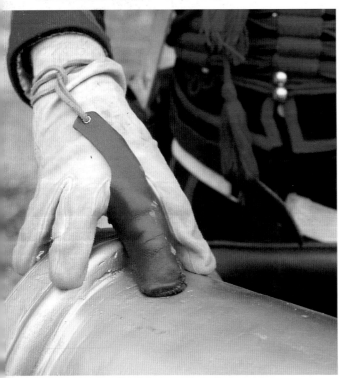

Horse Artillery crew, in the light cavalry style uniform of that branch and the shako of c.1810 onwards, loading a field piece. In reality the crew would consist of at least six, often eight gunners, plus a number of infantrymen to manhandle the gun and to keep a supply of ammunition coming briskly from the caisson. In battle, of course, casualties often reduced the crew and forced men to "double up" their duties. We number these gunners as if a full crew were present:

(Above) The No.2 man, standing right of the muzzle, swabs the barrel with the wetted sponge to extinguish any powder sparks or smouldering fragments of cartridge before the next charge is loaded. It was very important to swab thoroughly, and fatally easy - under the pressure of battle - to become careless, with gruesome consequences when the swabber came to ram the new charge home.

(Left) During the swabbing and ramming the ventsman standing left of the breech - No.4 in the crew - keeps his finger (protected by a leather stall) over the vent or touchhole to prevent any rush of air fanning sparks into life.

(Right) The loader, No.3, take the next round from one of the ammunition carriers, and place it in the muzzle.

The usual ammunition fired at long and medium ranges wa "roundshot", a solid iron ball. This was normally made up into "fixed" ammunition: it wa fixed to a wooden disc (*sabot*) with a bag holding the powder charge attached to the other side.

(Left) No.2 now reverses his staff and uses the solid wooden rammer end to force the round home. Here No.3 is helping him. Some rammer staffs bore marks to help remind the gunners if there was already a round in the gun - strange as it seems, even well-drilled men could make such straight-forward mistakes in the confusion of battle.

(Above) The shot was attached to the sabot by tin straps and brass tacks, and the bag was tied or tacked in place. This cartridge was made of flannel or serge, which burned away almost completely when the charge ignited. The usual powder charge was from a quarter to a third of the ball weight. Fixed ammunition made for a quicker rate of fire (about twice per minute under battle conditions), and much greater safety than handling loose powder.

The main alternative load was canister shot - this was a cylindrical tin holding (depending on calibre and required range) between 28 and 112 iron balls, also fixed to a cartridge bag. This was lethal against formed infantry and cavalry at close range; the tin burst at the muzzle, spreading the balls in a cone 32 feet across at 100 yards from the gun. The deadliest load of all was a roundshot with a canister rammed in on top.

(Right) No.4 thrusts a brass pricker down the vent to pierce the powder bag. He then inserts a fuze or firing tube - *étapille* - down the vent and into the pierced cartridge.

The NCO in command of the gun, No.1, will now aim by levering the end of the tra right or left by means of a handspike - a wooden bar inserted in metal brackets - and if necessary adjusting the range by means of the elevating screw under the breech.

(Left) The elevating screw. Cannon were not fired at much above horizontal in open field battles; roundshot fired at flat trajectory first grazed the ground at between 300 and 600 metres, then ricochetted to hit again at between 550 and 1,100m (depending upon many variables, e.g. weight, charge, wind, state of the ground, etc.). The gunner, judging by eye and experience, tried to make his ball arrive at the target below man-height above the ground.

(Above) No.1 now applies the portfire - a short staff with burning quickmatch fixed to the end - to the fuze; and the gun will fire. If the match needs relighting he will carry it to a smouldering slowmatch kept a safe distance from the gun and ammunition. In reality the gunner and chest seen here behind the trail would be further away and outside the line of the wheels - guns recoil sharply when fired with a full load.

(Above right) As well as bein deafening (the sound of their own guns firing was thought t encourage conscripts), the smoke and flame of a battery firing was an impressive sight and an intimidating one for the enemy. French artillerymen were renowned for their accuracy; and luckily for them nearly all their opponents arrayed their lines and column in the open (with the significant exception of the Duke of Wellington, who always tried to keep his men under cover until the last moment). At Eylau in 1807 a British observer wrote that "The French cannon quickly replied with vigour and effect as every man of the Russian army was exposed from head to heel". A ball ploughing int close-packed ranks did dreadful damage; the greatest carnage seen by one officer was 26 killed or wounded by one shot at Waterloo.

(Right) Dragging the gun bac into position after it has recoiled. An 8-pdr. weighed nearly a ton, a 12-pdr. nearly twice that.

(**Above & left**) On a bridge between Champaubert and Montmirail during the re-enacted Campaign of France, a Horse Artillery crew wait to serve hot canister to advancing troops of the King's German Legion. Campaign covers and cloaks protect them not only from rain and chill, but also from the black, sludgy residue of burnt and wetted powder. Manning a black powder cannon is a filthy job - and a dangerous one: burnt hands and faces, and crushed fingers and toes, were characteristic marks of veteran gunners.

(**Right**) Reconstruction of a Horse Artillery guidon.

(Left) A smartly turned-out gunner showing off the red-frogged hussar-style dolman jacket, tight breeches with thigh braiding, and light cavalry boots. He has laid aside his red and blue barrel sash and sabre belt.

(Below left & below) In 1812 regulations stipulated the replacement of the dolman by a simpler habit-veste, but this red-laced waistcoat preserves something of the old look; as always, surviving contemporary drawings show a wide variety of details. Pantalons à cheval *("charivari")* were also ordered, with black leather inserts to reinforce the cloth and increase their useful life. The scarlet stripe edged an opening down the outer seam closed by 18 brass buttons, so that the overalls could be put on and taken off over the breeches without removing the boots.

(Right) An impressive reconstruction of a general officer of Imperial Guard Hor Artillery wearing a hussar-sty uniform of superb quality.

The fur colpack has gold
ords, a gold-embroidered
carlet *flamme* or bag, and a
eather plume - white
as the colour for staff posts
every level of command in
apoleon's army.

The general's dolman, with
ve rows of gilt ball buttons,
d the tight Hungarian-style
reeches, are cut from
perfine blue cloth of a rich
ade, and lavishly
mbroidered and frogged
ith gold lace and cord, the
ain elements edged with
ne tracery. This decoration
carried round onto the rear
both dolman and breeches.
he number of strips of gold
ce at forearm and thigh, and
e silver metal stars applied
the sleeve lace, mark his
nk.

Beneath the red and gold
rrel sash his sabre belt

and slings are of finest red
Morocco leather embroidered
with bullion thread, the
gilt buckle plates and bosses
decorated with lion masks.
The sabretache is of
matching leather, the flap
richly decorated with gold
lace and bullion embroidery
incorporating crossed
cannon, and repeating the
three applied silver stars of
rank. His hussar-cut boots
have gold lace edge trim and
tassels.

In the face of all this
magnificence one final point
is perhaps worth making: on
a Napoleonic battlefield this
god of war stood in just as
much danger of being
stretched dead in the filth as
was the grubby gunner with
whom we close this book
overleaf.